Bibliographic information published by the German National Library:

The German National Library lists this publication in the National Bibliography; detailed bibliographic data are available on the Internet at http://dnb.dnb.de .

Imprint:

Copyright © 2016 GRIN Verlag, Open Publishing GmbH
Print and binding: Books on Demand GmbH, Norderstedt Germany
ISBN: 9783668309067

This book at GRIN:

http://www.grin.com/en/e-book/340983/social-networks-an-analysis-of-vk-com

Mihail Novichkov

Social Networks. An analysis of VK.com

GRIN Publishing

GRIN - Your knowledge has value

Since its foundation in 1998, GRIN has specialized in publishing academic texts by students, college teachers and other academics as e-book and printed book. The website www.grin.com is an ideal platform for presenting term papers, final papers, scientific essays, dissertations and specialist books.

Visit us on the internet:

http://www.grin.com/

http://www.facebook.com/grincom

http://www.twitter.com/grin_com

Analysis of the VK* social network

*VK is the largest European online social networking service. It is based in St. Petersburg.[4] It is available in several languages, but is especially popular among Russian-speaking users

Objective:

To create a theory and software for extracting features out of the text information from the walls of social network users and then to group them by their interests.

Possible applications:

1. Improvement of the algorithms,which predicts information diffusion.

2. Advertising in social networks

3. Creation of databases or similar users

4. Promotion in social networks

This file consists of 3 parts:

1. Theory

2. Test run

3. Run on a real network user

References:

[1] Illustrative Mathematical Statistics. (M.B.Lagutin)
[2] Topic modeling in BigARTM: theory, algorithms, applications. (K.V.Vorontsov)
[3] Verification of the hypotheses about the distribution uniformity and symmetry for multidimensional data. (N.K.Bakirov)
[4] http://www.machinelearning.ru/
[5] Additive Regularization of Topic Models for Topic Selection and Sparse Factorization (K.V.Vorontsov)

(The work is designed for people, who are familiar with Topic modeling theory, otherwise please read article [5])

Theory

Introduction to the work:

In today's world, millions of people every day, getting up from the bed in the morning and the first thing come to their page and travel through the social network. With time the page collects a lot of information. Information about the habits, interests, hobbies, political views - all in one degree or another is deposited on the user's page. Some people do not even think what kind of informative trail they leave in social networks.

The idea of this work is to analyze one of the sources of information and on the basis of this data, to combine users into categories and give researchers the opportunity to study the characteristics of a group. As a source of information, we will take the wall of a user of the social network.

(This work was created as a tool to study the social network user environment, but in fact can be used in different applications and for different purposes. The generated code can be quickly reoriented to analyze the content of other social networks or sources of information.)

Approximations and idea of the study:

The first approximation of the work will consist in the fact that we will identify a user with the information on the wall of his account. Of course, this is not entirely correct, because there are many other modalities, which also carry information, but in this work, they will be ignored.

The second approximation of the work is associated with the approximations used in the algorithms of BigARTM, such as a bag-of-words, for example. More information about the complete list of of these approximations can be found in [2].

After a few experiments with vector models, I came to the conclusion that they were not very applicable to assess the degree of similarity. So I turned to a more powerful tool for text analysis, namely the topic model, which after a few trial runs immediately showed its ability to allocate the interpreted topics from a given set of texts.

Hence the idea: Each user will be characterized by its own distribution over topics.

After constructing a topic model, the matrices Φ and Θ will appear in the hands of researchers , the second of which will be the matrix of the object/topics. Upon receipt of the matrix Θ the researcher gets the regular task of clustering.

Next, we will describe each step of the in more detail work.

The texts source :

Each account of a social network has dedicated place where the owner of the account and his friends can write messages. This place is called the "wall". Each document of the processed collection represents the first 100 records from the wall of a friend of the investigated user of the social network. As a result, our collection consists of the texts from the walls of the accounts of the friends of the investigated users. The number 100 was chosen because the VK API does not allow to download more records from the wall of one account.

Sometimes a user does not allow the application to view his wall, so the final number of documents is the number of friends minus those who banned to explore their walls.

The texts preprocessing:

After the first construction of a topic model it becomes clear that preprocessing of the text in this case is not quite usual. Those works that came to me during my preparation, used the standard stemmer and lists of stop- words from a standard library (for example, SnowballStemmer). In the case of social networks, this approach is hardly applicable because of the huge amounts of slang stop words which are not included in the standard lists. So we had to make our own list of stop words. But creating a good list of stop words for social networks is a big job, one man is not enough for a such task, so it is better to use crowd sourcing for filling the list .

Topic model development:

This item is best to start with substantiation the choice of the regularizators and the coefficients to them.

In this project 4 regularizators were chosen, namely - sparsing of Φ, sparsing of Θ , decorrelator of Θ and topic selection.

Sparcing of Φ and Θ were chosen to meet the sparseness hypothesis (as for the implementation of subsequent clustering the fact that the matrices are sparse can be an advantage), and to reduce the entropy of the distribution.

Decorrelator Θ was chosen because, after clustering the researcher must answer the question, what topic unites each cluster. Decorrelator Θ contributes to various topics, thus making it easier to the researcher to perform his task.

As described in [2] and [4], automatic correction of regularization strategies is an open problem of machine learning, , therefore I used the strategy which was performed in [5].

"Decorrelation coefficient grows linearly during the first 60 iterations up to the highest value $\gamma = 200000$ that does not deteriorate the model. Topic selection with $\tau = 0.3$ is turned on later, after the 15-th iteration. Topic selection and decorrelation are used at alternating iterations because their effects may conflict. To get rid of insignificant words in topics and to prepare insignificant topics for further elimination, sparsing is turned on staring from the 40-th iteration. Its coefficients α_t, β_w gradually increase to zeroize 2% of Θ elements and 9% of Φ elements each iteration. As a result, we get a sequence of models with decreasing number of sparse interpretable domain-specific topics."

4

The clustering algorithm:

Ideal or better clustering algorithms do not exist.According to [1], with a large number of objects we should choose fast hierarchical procedures for reductive measures of distance. Therefore, Ward's hierarchical algorithm method has been chosen as the clustering algorithm. It is also stated in [1], that the algorithm we have chosen seemed to the author to be the best method for recoverability of the partition.

The problem of unknown number of clusters:

Upon receipt of the dendrogram it is necessary to decide how to draw the line to get the most plausible number of clusters. In this paper we propose the following approach to solve this problem.

In each node of the dendrogram there is a division of a set of objects in 2 subsets. In order to decide if this step is necessary or not, it is proposed to test the data of each node for uniformity.

According to [3], the following algorithm is to be applied to check the uniformity/homogeneity of multivariate data:

1. Let's consider the node k

2. Suppose that all the left leaves of the node k make the set of $X = \{x_1, x_2, ..., x_n\}$

3. Suppose that all the right leaves of the node k make the set of $Y = \{y_1, y_2, ..., y_m\}$

4. Suppose that $S_1 = \frac{1}{n^2} \sum_{i,j=1}^{n} |x_i - x_j|$

5. Suppose that $S_2 = \frac{1}{m^2} \sum_{i,j=1}^{n} |y_i - y_j|$

6. Suppose that $S_2 = \frac{1}{mn} \sum_{i=1}^{n} \sum_{j=1}^{m} |x_i - y_j|$

5

7. If $Q = 1 - \frac{S_1 + S_2}{2S3} = 0$, then the test is passed. Otherwise, the test is not passed.

Each subtree, passed the test, we will paint in one color. Then, it is easy to draw a line on the dendrogram to separate the clusters in a most reasonable way.

Due to the fact that the uniformity/homogeneity test in the form presented above, was derived for the sets of X, Y which contain large number of elements, the test is not always applicable in practice. The practice has shown that the test can be considered passed if $Q \leqslant 0.2$

Summary:

After performing the algorithm/items described above, the researcher receives on hands the matrix people/topics/clusters. Operating with this matrix, we can find answers to questions about our environment in a social network

Test run

In this section we show the results of the algorithm on an account specially created in the VK social network.

The following 9 people have been added as friends to the account:

Politicians:

Unus-Bek Evkurov - leader of Ingushetia
Sergey Mironov - leader of the political party "Fair Russia"
Dmitry Medvedev - Russian Prime Minister
Ramzan Kadyrov - head of the Chechen Republic

Foxford professors:

Mikhail Penkin – the 1st year physics professor
Imran Alkeskerov - the 2nd year physics professor

Russian rap singers

Stas Konchenkov
Big Russian Boss

Fighters:

Buvaisar Saitiev - multiple Olympic champion in freestyle wrestling

For familiarization please see below the graph perplexity/iterations:

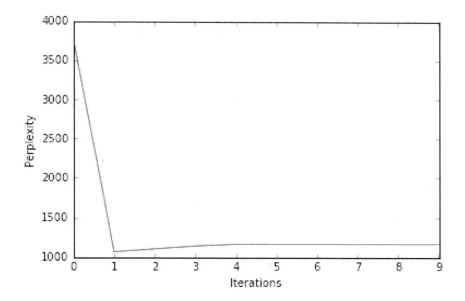

We see that the matrices have converged per 1 iteration.

Please see the resulting dendrogram below.

It is reasonable to assume that the algorithm should divide people by occupation.

In this case, we know the number of clusters (4) in advance, and it will

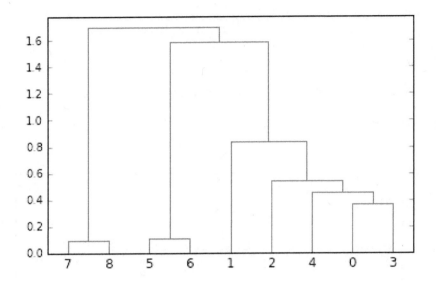

not be difficult to draw the line (for example, $D = 0.6$).

Let us see, in which clusters the friends of the test account fell.

As we can see from the matrix below, in this example, the algorithm worked well as a diagonal matrix is obtained.

Some topics are especially characteristic of certain clusters. For example, topic number 0 is particularly characteristic for the rap singers, and topic number 5 is typical for the teachers.

Let us take a look at them:

(All images are on the next page)

cluster	names	real
3	Юнус-Бек Евкуров	politic
4	Бувайсар Сайтиев	fighter
3	Сергей Миронов	politic
3	Дмитрий Медведев	politic
3	Рамзан Кадыров	politic
2	Стас Конченков	rap singer
2	Big Russian Boss	rap singer
1	Михаил Пенкин	foxford
1	Имран Алескеров	foxford

	foxford	rap singer	politic	fighter
0	2	0	0	0
1	0	2	0	0
2	0	0	4	0
3	0	0	0	1

Rap singers	Professors
god	portal
release	will receive
rap	masterclass
single	telephone
album	black
hard	atom

It is evident that the topics are interpretable.

Run on the real network user

In this section we try to analyze a real network user account.

As an example we take the account of my classmate, who kindly allowed me to use it.

For familiarization please see below the graph perplexity/iterations:

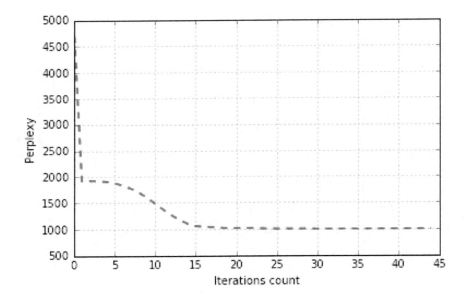

If we will have a look at the heatmap of the matrix Θ we will see that all topics are very sparse.

Let us look at the interpretability of some topics:

topic4:	topic5:	topic6:	topic8:	topic12:
Film	phystech	minutes	schoool	words
Concert	mipt	test	professor	press
Ticket	olympiad	sugar	play	muscle
student	was given	spoon	student	kilos
club	course	ready	lesson	approach
competition	tasks	cheese	books	feet

The table above shows that:
Topic 1 is dedicated to visits to the movies, theater
Topic 5 is dedicated to the MIPT university.
Topic 6 is dedicated to recipes
Topic 8 is dedicated to school and the associated events
Topic 12 is dedicated to athletes in the gym

We construct a dendrogram and paint it in accordance with the results of the homogeneity test on its nodes.

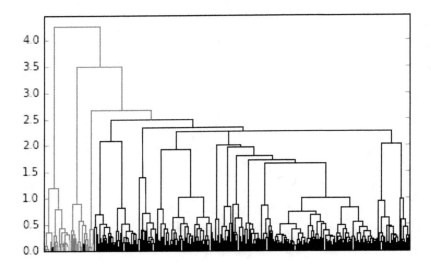

We can see that more than half of the friends are alike. Let us place the boundary so that the monochrome segment is divided minimally, but provided that big leaps of distances ($D = 1.5$).are cut off. A total of 16 clusters came out.

After this step, we obtain the matrix people/features/clusters. Analyzing the resulting matrix allows us to answer a variety of questions about the environment in the social network. For example we can calculate the the group of people who are most interested in the university (MIPT). Let us get 4 most vivid representatives of the group, in which the average percentage of topic 5 (MIPT) occurrence is the highest, and see who people really are.

Results:

Mikhail Penkin – MIPT professor

Shamil Musin - MIPT Youth Committee member

Evgeny Chernyavsky - MIPT professor

Oleg Ermakov – representative of the 3d year the Management and Applied Mathematics Faculty in the student council.

We can see that the algorithm has given the people who are directly connected with the university.

Summary:

Based on of the experiments performed I think that the algorithm is applicable in practice. However, there is space for improvement and development, namely: improving the list of stop words, setting more intelligent regularization strategy of the model, identification and removal of the stop-topics, which do not characterize the user of a social network (for example, the topic of birthday greetings).

: